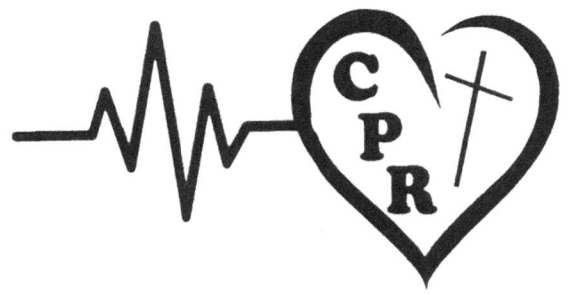

CPR FOR THE BELIEVER

Life Changing Principles for a Quality Life

Steve Feazel

© 2018 by Steve Feazel
All Rights Reserved.

No part of this publication may be reproduced, stored in a retrieval system, or transmitted, in any form or by any means, electronic, mechanical, photocopying, recording, or otherwise, without the written permission of the author.

First published by Dog Ear Publishing
4011 Vincennes Road
Indianapolis, IN 46268
www.dogearpublishing.net

ISBN: 978-145756-759-9

All scripture is from the NIV unless otherwise stated

The Holy Bible, New International Version,® NIV® Copyright © 1973, 1978, 1984, 2011 by Biblica, Inc.™ Used by Permission. All rights reserved worldwide. *New International Version* Published by Zondervan Grand Rapids, Michigan 49530, USA

Endorsements

Being Consistent, Persistent and Resistant to the temptation to fall short in these areas hurts one's spiritual life. Most of my prayers for my personal life and ministry focus on these very points. No matter how deep our faith, how strong our relationship is with God, we can all use a little CPR (consistence, persistence, and resistance) to support us on our walk with Him. I appreciate Steve Feazel's work in providing us a framework for that support and the reminder that CPR breathes life into us as we follow Christ.

> Melissa Ohden, Abortion Survivor, Author and Prominent Pro-Life Speaker

CPR for the Believer, "Consistent, Persistent and Resistant," is a great little book for reviving the spiritual energy for Christians who have allowed their faith walk to become lethargic. It is sure to become a favorite for many Christians.

> Dr. Carol M. Swain, Author, Speaker, Professor of Law & Political Science at Vanderbilt University (Ret.) and frequent guest on the Fox News Channel

For each of us in our Christian lives there is a time when we all need something to motivate us to move to a deeper and more effective walk with the Lord. This book is that something. It deepens your relationship with Christ and will help your spirit soar to new heights. A great encouragement and a must read!

> Tim Throckmorton, Midwest Regional Director for Church Ministries, Family Research Council

The three words - consistent, persistent, and resistant are foundational attributes, which are important in almost any pursuit, whether one is building a business, raising a family, pursuing a goal, or facing a challenge in life. Steve Feazel builds a compelling case that these concepts are particularly important for individuals seeking to faithfully follow Christ. *CPR for the Believer: Life Changing Principles for a Quality Life* is a helpful guide for young and old alike. The book is filled with engaging illustrations and clear points of application. This is also an effective tool to pass along to others who are seeking a closer walk with the Lord.

> Dr. John C. Bowling, President, Olivet Nazarene University

Attention to the Consistent, Persistent, and Resistant strategies for spiritual depth in our time is desperately needed. Steve Feazel provides a clear path for anyone who desires to maintain or rekindle a strong spiritual life. I recommend this book to anyone who is serious about cultivating a deeper spiritual walk.

> Dr. Henry Spaulding II, President, Mount Vernon Nazarene University

CPR for the Believer is such a practical and powerful book. It is easily read, easily understood and easily applicable. You will find a wealth of practical truth based wholly on scripture that will help you to resuscitate your walk with Christ.

> Bob Burney, Radio Talk Show Host, of Salem Radio Network in Columbus, Ohio (WRFD)

Dedication

To my wife, Edythe

Contents

Foreword xiii

Introduction 1

Chapter 1: Consistent: Keeping a Constant
Relationship with Christ 7

Chapter 2: Persistent: Staying the Course of Your
Calling 27

Chapter 3: Resistant: Standing Strong against
Temptation 59

Chapter 4: Application: Utilizing the Divine
Guidance System 83

Endnotes 99

Acknowledgements 102

Foreword

Understanding what the Bible and the Christian life is all about can be a daunting and confusing task for many people today. Then a book like *The Prayer of Jabez* by Bruce Wilkinson comes along to clarify practical Biblical principles and thousands of people find it to be very helpful for their personal lives. Many listen to sermons, read books, or go to conferences hoping to be more effective in living out their faith in everyday life. And yet, a month later they cannot remember even one principle they have learned. What we need are memory hooks that can remind us of the biblical concepts we need to apply to our current life situations we are facing.

This is what I really like about Steve Feazel's new book, *CPR for the Believer*. We are all familiar with the abbreviation CPR. It is synonymous with providing emergency assistance for someone who is having a serious heart or breathing crisis. Steve Feazel has taken those same three letters, CPR, to remind us as Christians what we need to be doing to maintain a healthy, growing personal faith. These letters stand for: Consistent, Persistent, and Resistant. This book fleshes out the personal meanings of these three key words and how we can apply them to our daily lives.

There are four key things that make this book effective:

1. It is brief. One could easily read it in one to three settings. It quickly gets to the heart of the chapter topic so one can grasp the concept and apply it to one's current situation.

2. It is practical. The emphasis of each chapter is how one implements the key word into daily living. This stuff works where the rubber meets the road where we all live.

3. It is understandable. Each chapter has multiple scripture passages that speak directly to the biblical understanding of the principle. There are illustrations from Bible characters, people from history, and contemporary situations that help the reader say, "Oh, I get it now."

4. It is memorable. Self-help books are not all that helpful if you can't remember later what the author was saying. The three words: consistent, persistent, and resistant, can be trigger words to help the reader be reminded

of what God wants us to be. You can have those three words on a wrist band, on your refrigerator, or on the dashboard of your car. It's a gentle reminder of the way God wants us to be living and growing.

I have been a friend of Steve Feazel from college and seminary days. We have pastored together and worked together on projects many times across the years. One of Steve's greatest desires in his writing and video projects is to make the Christian life understandable and practical. When you read this book you will be struck by the fact that these three concepts are at the same time simple and profound. In the end you will say, this is the way the Christian life is meant to be lived.

Dr. Bruce Petersen, D. Min.

Professor of Pastoral Ministry (Ret.)

Mount Vernon Nazarene University

Introduction

The letters "C P R" are familiar to us in the context of the lifesaving procedure used when someone goes into cardiac arrest. The letters CPR stand for Cardiopulmonary Resuscitation. It is a procedure where the chest is compressed and air is blown in the airways of a person who is experiencing a heart attack. My father had to be resuscitated when he had a heart attack. It allowed him to be alive for by-pass surgery that gave him more years of life. People can take lessons to learn how to properly give CPR. Every church would be wise to have someone in their congregation with this skill.

I have been an ordained minister for over 48 years. During that time I have served as associate pastor, senior pastor, in a position with a para-church organization and in a post at a Christian college. This has given me opportunities to observe Christians living out their faith in various circumstances. I have noticed that many encounter great frustration in reaching the full potential of the spiritual life God has available for them. Many are very inconsistent in their own spiritual growth and fall short more times than not of rendering fruitful service for God's kingdom.

Now in retired status as a minister, but far from being retired from ministry, I have reflected on what actually is the key to spiritual victory or a life that meets the desire that Jesus has for us. It needs to be rediscovered and embraced, so that as Christians we can be the people Christ wants us to be and fulfill the mission he has for us.

The evangelical church is badly hemorrhaging as membership shrinks in many churches. In those churches where attendance has soared, true active discipleship has waned. God has so much available to us, but we choose not to take advantage of it both to our loss and that of the world. This book will focus on a simple concept that can place one's spiritual life back on track where the abundant life Christ has in store for a Christian can be realized.

I call this concept "CPR for the believer." I believe that many Christians need their spiritual lives resuscitated to revitalize their personal relationship with Christ and the churches they attend. The three letters stand for "Consistent, Persistent and Resistant." I believe that spiritual failure or malaise takes place in one or more of these three areas of a Christian's life. This book will examine these three areas and ascertain their importance to living a victorious Christian life.

Often Christians become so busy in church work and with their daily responsibilities that life becomes about doing instead of being. It becomes a struggle to maintain a regular time of personal fellowship with the Lord where prayer and the study of Scripture recharge the spirit. Consistency is needed or one becomes vulnerable to the advances of the enemy of the soul.

Getting the Fundamentals Right

In our rapid-paced world, we like to see quick results. Impatience is a common affliction that infects many Christians. The work that God sets before us is not always accomplished in the time frame we desire, but we must not give up, especially when we know the work is his will for us. We must stay persistent and keep true to the call and stay the course.

My father was big on fundamentals. When I played little league baseball he taught me how to throw by teaching me the fundamentals of stretching my arm out behind me then bringing it forward in a semi-circle instead of just bringing the ball up by my ear and throwing it. His way gave me more power in throwing from my center field position. He also gave me valuable fundamentals when he taught me to drive including how to change a tire. One time in my childhood, we had my newly married cousin and her husband for Thanksgiving dinner. My cousin made the pumpkin pie. My dad took one bite and said, "Shirley, what did you not put in this pie?" She tasted it and said, "Oh no, I forgot the sugar!"

Fundamentals are important, be it on the athletic field, the highway or in the kitchen. Many churches function far below their potential because they have a number of people who have neglected the key fundamentals of Christian life. This book sends out an alert for them to return to these fundamentals and become spiritually healthy once more and effective in service for Christ.

We are involved in a spiritual war. When you are at war, you have an enemy. We have a very powerful one in Satan, but we have one on our side who is more powerful. We will be tested and tempted to give up the fight, but we dare not if we hope for spiritual victory in this life and glory in the next. We must resist the enemy's temptations that would spell certain defeat for our souls.

A Simple Concept

CPR for the Christian life is a very simple concept – Consistent, Persistent and Resistant. These three words form a tri-point focus for personal spiritual inspection. My hope is that while you study these three spiritual factors in the following pages, you will feel the presence of the Holy Spirit who will enrich your insight. God has entrusted us to advance his kingdom on earth. If your spiritual health is poor, you will fail miserably. This book can be an aid to improve your spiritual vitality. You may actually find it resuscitating your soul.

Consistent

Keeping a Constant Relationship with Christ

Consistency is highly valued in our society. We want our sports teams to be consistent. We are frustrated when one week they play fantastic and win a big game and then the next week play below par and lose to an inferior opponent. If you are an employer, you want employees who are consistent in their work and attendance. Exceptional work one day, followed by disinterest and preventable mistakes the next is not acceptable. No boss likes unreliable attendance by an employee. If we value consistency, it only stands to reason that God also values it, and wants it from us.

The letter "C" in *CPR for the Believer* stands for *consistent*. Our relationship with Christ must be consistent as we fellowship with him through the Holy Spirit. This consistent connection transcends a daily quiet time of personal devotions where Bible reading and prayer are experienced. There are days when these times can become mechanical, where we seem to be going through the motions without any real bonding with the Lord. But this time should never be neglected, for very often it is the moment when our spirit links with Christ's spirit.

Being More Than a Fan

Kyle Idleman wrote a profound book entitled, *Not a Fan*. The premise of the book is that many who take the name Christian are more like fans of Jesus rather than true followers. He writes in the book, "When we decide to believe in Jesus without making a commitment to follow him, we become nothing more than fans.[1]

To be consistent in living the Christian life is to live as a true follower of Christ where we allow him to remake us in his spiritual image. We become "Christlike." Paul wrote in Philippians 2:5, "Your attitude should be the same as that of Christ Jesus." This is a very high expectation for a Christian. It cannot be obtained by a fickle devotion to the Lord.

Peter echoes Paul's concept of a Jesus make-over when he writes in 2 Peter 1:4, "… he has given us his very great and precious promises, so that through them you may participate in the divine nature, having escaped the corruption in the world caused by evil desires." These promises include his daily guidance, his unconditional love and eternal life.

Being able to participate in the divine nature is an extraordinary opportunity for mere mortals, but Jesus gives this fantastic opportunity to us. It is not something developed in Christian fans, only in true followers. To be spiritually consistent is to personally connect with Christ in some way daily where our spirit interacts with his spirit. There becomes a sense in our hearts that we have met and been impacted by Jesus' character.

Often this happens in prayer or reading the scriptures. It may also happen through spiritual music or in conversation with a fellow Christian who has become a trusted friend and encourager. It can be as simple as just having the sense of his presence as you have a worshipful thought. The key is that every day your soul is being touched by Jesus Christ because you want it to be, and you willingly keep the channels open for Jesus to do just that.

When you live like this you are developing a consistent spiritual walk with the Lord where you have unbroken fellowship with Jesus Christ, and it paves the way for spiritual excitement that will exceed your expectation. The focus of life is God's will over self-will. Jesus was the great example in this. He was all about doing the will of his Father, even when it meant being the sin offering on the cross.

Danger of the Elevator Ride

The difficulty of keeping a consistent fellowship with the Lord is the battle of the will. We are to want and seek God's will, this we know, but there always seem to be those crooked side trails from the straight and narrow way that we end up taking for a while to satisfy some selfish interest.

The Christian life becomes an up and down elevator ride instead of a purposeful walk on a divinely designed corridor. The Apostle Peter experienced this elevator ride during his days as a disciple. He boldly proclaimed to Jesus that he believed him to be the Christ, which is the Messiah. He later denied this Messiah three times before the rooster crowed.

He stepped out of the boat to walk on water with his Master until his lack of faith took him down to where Jesus had to be his lifeline. Peter had a problem with spiritual consistency. Actually, all of the disciples did as they scattered when Jesus was crucified. Their consistency did not take hold until Pentecost.

We have more timesaving devices than the world has ever known in its history, but still we manage to not have enough time to do all we want. So many Christians live lives not in overdrive, but in overload. There are responsibilities with work, with family and the church. We then acquire a number of add-ons, the soccer practice for the kids, the volunteer service for some worthy charity, the pursuit of a personal hobby and whatever other tantalizing item drifts before us.

We become busy with so many good things in life that it becomes difficult to be a true follower or disciple of Christ. We willingly divide our lives into fragments. We are stressing out trying to sew them together in some acceptable format that will allow us to cope with it all.

Timesaving gadgets give us more time to do what we want to do. Maybe that's the problem. The focus of our lives should be not on what we want to do, but on what we know God wants us to be, or what he wants us to do. We are so caught up in our results oriented world that we think the essence of life is to achieve some great results, when Jesus is saying, "Just come to me and give me your life and I will make you over in my character."

When Jesus called Peter and Andrew to be his disciples, he said, "Come, follow me and I will make you fishers of men." Jesus didn't say how many men they would catch, because his focus was on them being followers that would bring about their total transformation.

In Galatians 5:7, Paul writes, "You were running a good race. Who cut in on you to keep you from obeying the truth?" Something happened in the spiritual walk of these Galatians. There was an interruption in their spiritual lives that took them off course. They were not being consistent in obeying the truth. They had a break in their fellowship with Jesus. Consequently, they were led astray by someone preaching a false doctrine.

Today, many Christians depart the way because of something not someone. That desired possession, that lofty position, that extra dollar or that extra add-on that promises an extra thrill. A wise man once said, "The surest way to have an empty life is to fill it full of things."

Jesus said, "No one can serve two masters. Either you will hate the one and love the other, or you will be devoted to the one and despise the other. You cannot serve both God and money." (Matthew 6:24) We can also add, "You cannot follow God's will and your own will."

Lukewarmness Doesn't Cut It

2 Chronicles 25:2 is a verse describing one of the kings of Judah named Amaziah. It says of him, "He did what was right in the eyes of the Lord, but not wholeheartedly."

Could that verse be used to describe you? Are you attending church, doing good things in the ministry of the church, and even giving money in the offering, but not doing it all wholeheartedly? This king of Judah was not the only one who had this problem in the Bible. We have the words of the Lord to one of the churches in Revelation:

Revelation 3:14-16

[14] "To the angel of the church in Laodicea write:

These are the words of the Amen, the faithful and true witness, the ruler of God's creation. [15] I know your deeds, that you are neither cold nor hot. I wish you were either one or the other! [16] So, because you are lukewarm—neither hot nor cold—I am about to spit you out of my mouth."

Lukewarmness is unacceptable to Jesus Christ. What does lukewarmness look like today? Pastor and author, Francis Chan, gives provocative insight into this in his book, *Crazy Love,* in the chapter called "Profile of the Lukewarm." He presents a number of descriptions of lukewarm Christians. Here are the four that stood out to me:

1. Lukewarm people tend to choose what is popular over what is right when they are in conflict. They desire to fit in both at church and outside the church; they care more about what people think of their actions (like church attendance and giving) than what God thinks of their hearts and lives.[2]

2. Lukewarm people say they love Jesus, and He is indeed, a part of their lives. But only a part. They give him a section of their time, their money, and their thoughts, but he isn't allowed to control their lives.[3]

3. Lukewarm people think about life on earth much more often than eternity in heaven. Daily life is mostly focused on today's to-do-list, this week's schedule, and next month's vacation. Rarely, if ever do they intently consider the life to come.[4]

4. Lukewarm people are continually concerned with playing it safe; they are slaves to the god of control. This focus on safe living keeps them from sacrificing and risking for God.[5]

Pastor Chan goes on to explain how he became convicted in his life that he was offering God leftovers. He committed to becoming a true disciple. If we are living consistent, dedicated lives to Christ, we move from lukewarm and give our best even when it becomes a challenge for us to do so. We live by faith and we do it consistently on a daily basis as God is faithful to us.[6]

The Fruit Bearing Requirement

Jesus told the story of "The Sower" in the Gospel of Matthew, naming the four soils receiving seeds: hard path, shallow, thorny and well prepared. The challenge presented by the thorny soil is relevant to our time. My wife and I live in the country. I can sit on my front porch in the summer and gaze out on a beautiful corn field or soybean field depending on the year.

My view from the back deck is different. It is a beautiful woods, but it is filled with thorny briar bushes some of which have reached out to greet me when I pass by on the riding-mower. No planted crops would fare well in this environment because the briar bushes would stunt their growth, verifying the words of Jesus when he explained the gospel seed falling among thorns, "The one who received the seed that fell among the thorns is the man who hears the word, but the worries of life and the deceitfulness of wealth choke it, making it unfruitful" (Matthew 13:22).

As a minister, I have seen new believers start on the Christian journey only to have the worries of life and the quests for material things wreck their faith. They began with Jesus, but they could not keep a consistent relationship with him.

On a trip to Florida to visit our grandchildren, my wife and I stayed at an Airbnb home which was the personal residence of the host family. We noticed scripture verses on signs stuck in the flower beds as we carried in our luggage. We thought how fortunate for us that this is a Christian home. The young host couple was vibrant in their Christian faith and we found them to be kindred spirits.

One evening the host wife asked me in her delightful Polish accent, "What is your favorite Scripture passage?" I don't recall ever being asked that question, but it did not take me long to reply. It is found in the Gospel of John and is commonly referred to as "The Vine and the Branches." I had preached from it numerous times. It is an illustration given by Jesus to his disciples revealing how important our Lord regards consistency when it comes to a relationship with him. Let's review the passage:

> [1] "I am the true vine, and my Father is the gardener. [2] He cuts off every branch in me that bears no fruit, while every branch that does bear fruit he prunes so that it will be even more fruitful. [3] You are already clean because of the word I have spoken to you. [4] Remain in me, as I also remain in you. No branch can bear fruit by itself; it must remain in the vine. Neither can you bear fruit unless you remain in me.
>
> [5] "I am the vine; you are the branches. If you remain in me and I in you, you will bear much fruit; apart from me you can do nothing. [6] If you do not remain in me, you are like a branch that is thrown away and withers; such branches are picked up, thrown into the fire and burned. [7] If you remain in me and my words remain in you, ask whatever you wish, and it will be done for you. [8] This is to my Father's glory, that you bear much fruit, showing yourselves to be my disciples. (John 15:1-8)

These verses describe the relationship that Christ's followers are to have with him. Jesus states that he is the vine and we are the branches, clearly revealing that we are subservient to him and dependent on him. A branch not connected to the vine withers and dies.

In verse five Jesus says, "If a man remains in me and I in him, he will bear much fruit." The word "remain" may also be translated "abide." Both words convey that it is necessary for a believer to stay consistently connected with Christ, which is essential to living a victorious Christian life.

In a vineyard, the vine provides the branches with the nourishment and substance needed for life so the branches can bear fruit. Jesus goes on to say, "... apart from me you can do nothing." These words are so true, but I believe many think they can do something apart from Christ. They are immersed in church activities and programs where they have mastered the routine and perform accordingly. They are doing what others see as good things, but there is no spiritual connection for them in the task. It is like the king we looked at earlier who did what was right in in the eyes of the Lord, but not wholeheartedly."

In verse one, Jesus introduces another personality, God the Father, as the gardener or owner of the vineyard. The Father is also concerned with consistency. A branch that is inconsistent in producing fruit is cut off and sent to destruction. The Father, as the gardener, also prunes. The word "disciple" comes from the word "discipline." A disciple of Jesus Christ must expect spiritual discipline.

When you become a true follower of Christ, you will experience spiritual pruning. When you bring your talent, time and treasure under his control, he will guide you to use all in an effective way that may require you to reprioritize certain areas of your life. If you are to remain in him, you will have to make the changes he asks of you.

What would it look like if an inconsistent life could be played out in the vineyard? A branch might be willing to attach to the vine for a while, depart for a self-interest excursion and then come back to be grafted into the vine. What quality of fruit would be produced? How desirable would that branch be to the Vine and to the Gardener?

The words of Jesus are very sobering in verse six: "If you do not remain in me, you are like a branch that is thrown away and withers; such branches are picked up, thrown into the fire and burned." Inconsistency in a relationship with Jesus can have devastating results.

A Remarkable Man of God

The Old Testament books of Kings and Chronicles give us the history of Israel through the reign of its kings and document Israel's inconsistency with God. They were the chosen people who chose to take wrong actions that broke their relationship and covenant with God to the point that

God's judgment allowed them to be carried off into captivity. The prophet Hosea was even told to take an adulterous wife so his life would be a reminder to Israel of their unfaithfulness to God and their inconsistency with him.

There is, however, a man called Job in the Old Testament who is a stellar example of consistency with God. Job was a devoted servant to God who was blessed with great wealth and a charmed life. One day the Lord and Satan had a conversation about Job:

> [8] Then the Lord said to Satan, "Have you considered my servant Job? There is no one on earth like him; he is blameless and upright, a man who fears God and shuns evil."
>
> [9] "Does Job fear God for nothing?" Satan replied. [10] "Have you not put a hedge around him and his household and everything he has? You have blessed the work of his hands, so that his flocks and herds are spread throughout the land. [11] But now stretch out your hand and strike everything he has, and he will surely curse you to your face."
>
> [12] The Lord said to Satan, "Very well, then, everything he has is in your power, but on the man himself do not lay a finger." Then Satan went out from the presence of the Lord. (Job 1:8-12)

A series of tragedies befell Job that resulted in the loss of his livestock, crops and his children who were killed in a storm. Then, Satan afflicted him with a painful disease of sores on his skin. Through all these misfortunes, Job stayed true to God. Job had three friends and a wife who advised him to give it up and curse God. In Job 13:15 (KJV) Job responds: "Though he slay me, yet will I trust in him…"

Job did not let his faith or relationship with God depend on circumstances. He passed the tests and stayed true to God. God restored his wealth to him, but Job did not expect this, because his real wealth was his relationship with God, and if that was all he had in life it would suffice.

A contemporary example of spiritual consistency is Billy Graham. His ministry impacted my life in an unusual way. In 1964, he held a crusade in my hometown of Columbus, Ohio. The call went out for people to be trained as counselors to work with those who would come forward to receive Christ at the crusade. I was a ministerial student between my freshman and sophomore year and I decided this would be a good experience, so I went for the training.

During one session I noticed an attractive young lady sitting in the pew in front of me. We talked during the break time, and agreed to sit together at the next session.

We began a friendship that went into courtship, over fifty years of marriage, two sons and four grandchildren. All of whom are happy that these two college kids sat together at a Billy Graham counselor training course.

Billy Graham was a remarkable man of God. One trait that stood out about him that was confirmed by so many was his humility. He did not seek to be famous or to achieve celebrity status. He only sought the will of God. When God chose to bless his ministry he never made it about himself.

He was solid in his study of God's word and in prayer. His message was simple. His passion for lost people was evident. My wife and I had the opportunity to visit his library in Charlotte, North Carolina. It is built in the shape of a barn, a link back to his days when he was raised on a farm.

As you walk through the various exhibits, you can hear excerpts from some of his sermons from different crusades and speaking events at college campuses. When you hear him voice that simple message of salvation, your spirit can discern the anointing of the Holy Spirit. The business side of his ministry was conducted with integrity and he never sought an extravagant lifestyle. Billy Graham had one goal, to live faithfully for God and do his will. He did just that. Billy Graham was consistent in his relationship with Jesus Christ. Because of it, he was an instrument that God used to bring others into his kingdom.

Richard A. Swenson is a medical doctor who wrote an insightful book, *Margin*, on the topic of overload that afflicts so many today in our hurry-up world. The book is so titled because the author believes we don't allow for margins in time, in finances, in emotions and other areas of life. We take everything to the max until one day the inevitable overload brings something crashing down. His words on the topic of time are most penetrating:

> The clock and Christ are not friends. Imagine what God thinks of us now that we are so locked into schedules that we have locked ourselves out of the Sermon on the Mount – it is hardly possible to walk the second mile today without offending one's pocket calendar. We jump at the alarm of a Seiko but sleep through the call of the Almighty.[7]

God doesn't use elevator Christians to touch the lives of others. The reliability is just not there. Hebrews 10:23 states, "Let us hold unswervingly to the hope we profess, for he who promised is faithful." That word "unswervingly" is very meaningful. It conveys that one is all-in and fully committed. Billy Graham sure was. We would do well to follow his example.

Consistency is Foundational

We can make this level of commitment because he who has made promises to us is faithful. Jesus has promised to be consistent to us. For all that he has done for us and promised to do in this life and the next, we need to be consistent for him and maintain an unbroken relationship. The Apostle Paul weighs in on this topic of consistent living with his words, " [16] Rejoice always, [17] pray continually, [18] give thanks in all circumstances; for this is God's will for you in Christ Jesus." (1 Thessalonians 5:16-18)

Paul believed that a Christian should rejoice always, pray continually and give thanks in all circumstances. This describes consistency in living for Christ. You may wonder what you must do to execute this lifestyle of spiritual consistency. First you have to really fall in love with Jesus Christ. You must know him as your savior and desire to cultivate his presence daily.

It is not something you can accomplish in your own strength but only through the Holy Spirit. A more detailed explanation of this will be presented in the final chapter since all three areas of the CPR for the believer require the Holy Spirit for effective application.

Consistency in a relationship with Jesus is important because it is foundational. The other areas, *persistence* and *resistance* that complete this CPR for the believer, are only successfully mastered when consistency is a reality.

Remember that being consistent with Jesus is touching his spirit with your spirit on a daily basis, where this encounter molds your disposition to be like that of our Lord himself. This makes it possible for you to mature in the faith and be someone through whom God can do wonderful things for his glory.

Discussion Questions: Chapter 1 Consistent

1. Kyle Idleman's concept of people being fans of Jesus and not real followers is very provocative. Do you believe it is a real issue for Christians today and if so, why?
2. In 2 Peter 1:4 we are told that we have the opportunity to participate in the divine nature. What does this mean to you?
3. Many Christians live the elevator experience of an inconsistent life as they seek to live their faith. What causes this and how can it be corrected?
4. Have you ever had a problem with spiritual lukewarmness? How did you overcome it?
5. In reference to the Vine and the Branches scripture passage, what fruit bearing should be expected of a Christian?
6. How is Dr. Swenson's concept of *Margin* relevant to the Christian life? How does it affect consistency in living the Christian life?
7. What gives you the most trouble in maintaining a consistent relationship with Jesus Christ?
8. What did you discover in this chapter about your walk with Christ that you would like to improve? What actions would be helpful for you to take?

2

Persistent

Staying the Course of Your Calling

In the previous chapter we looked at the importance of a personal relationship with Christ and how he wants to change us into his likeness. "Being" was given a higher priority than "doing." Consistency in our relationship with Christ is vital and foundational for successful Christian living. In this chapter, we focus on the second letter of CPR as it relates to the Christian life. The "P" is for *Persistent*. "Being" may be a higher priority than "doing," but that does not mean that "doing" is lightly regarded.

Jesus knew the execution of his mission would be difficult for his disciples and filled with obstacles. A strong spiritual character would be needed for success in his mission. Jesus said, [19] "Therefore go and make disciples of all nations, baptizing them in the name of the Father and of the Son and of the Holy Spirit, ..." (Matthew 28:19) This portion of the Great Commission clearly shows that Jesus is interested in the "doing" and was hopeful for results: more disciples that are real followers and not just fans. Disciples are charged with making other disciples.

This was the last instruction given to his disciples so we can conclude it was very important. However, few churches today have strong discipleship courses available for their members. True discipleship training has depth to it. It is not to be an easy process to complete and walk away from with a certificate that is shut in a drawer never to be seen again. It is designed to be an encounter with our Lord that will change your life and the way you live it. To become a disciple is to become a disciple maker.

As a follower of Christ, you will become involved in the mission of Christ. The Lord will, in a proper course of time, let you know what his will is for you in the service to his kingdom. You will be called to a task that will be your personal mission and he will expect you to embark on fulfilling it. To be successful you will have to be persistent. As you go about fulfilling the mission of Christ, you will experience joy and elation, but you will also encounter setbacks, disappointments and difficult trials. You will need to be persistent to overcome them.

Persistence means to continue steadfastly through whatever difficulties come your way. One of my favorite singing groups is the 2nd Chapter of Acts made up of Annie (Herring), Nelly (Greisen) and Matthew Ward. These siblings had a positive ministry in music from 1973 to 1988 that touched the hearts of millions. They became famous for their song about the resurrection of Christ called the *Easter Song*. On one of their albums they have a song entitled, *Takin' the Easy Way*. The song contains the lyrics:

> Takin' the easy way
> Isn't an easy way[1]

They remind us that if we are looking for an easy way in life, being a disciple of Jesus Christ is not it. We soon find out that any way that is not God's will, no matter how easy it appears, does not end up being easy.

We are conditioned for the easy in our society. The smart phone makes it easy to communicate to someone instantly from anywhere without even talking to them. The microwave makes lunch easy. Modern transportation makes travel easy. We even like church the easy way. We can just go to a mega-church and slip in and out without having to make any real commitment. When things get hard, we can just drop out. People do this. The job gets tough, just find another one. If the marriage has problems then divorce and remarry. Our society does not value persistence like God values it.

Overcoming Obstacles

Paul told the Galatians, "Let us not become weary in doing good, for at the proper time we will reap a harvest if we do not give up" (Galatians 6:9). God wants to make us winners. The only way we become losers is if we give up and quit. A famous entertainer was once asked, "What is the key to making it in show business?" His answer was "persistence." He went on to elaborate how he had met others along the way in his career with just as much talent or more, but who gave up the quest when the going got tough.

The late Vince Flynn was a bestselling author of CIA thrillers. When he took the leap to become a writer, he took a night job and wrote during the day. He finished his first novel entitled, *Term Limits*, but received sixty rejection letters. He took a daring step and self-published his book in his home area of Minneapolis-St. Paul. It became the number one seller in the Twin Cities which led to him receiving a two book deal from a Simon and Schuster imprint. More books followed as he established himself as a *New York Times* bestselling author until his life was cut short at the age of forty-seven from cancer.[2]

Vince did not give up even when the rejection letters came pouring in on him. He just became creative and found another way to reach his goal. This is the type of persistence we need in the task that God gives us.

I have a neighbor who is ninety-years-old at the writing of this book. As a young man, Jim worked as an engineer at a factory that made compressors. Jim had an idea for a small compressor that could deal with a number of problems faced by their customers. The large compressors made by the well-known company could not address these problems. He presented his idea and the company turned him down. He still believed his idea was sound so he started his own company to make the smaller compressor. It is now decades later and Jim has handed control of the company to his daughter. The company has made Jim a millionaire many times over, and he has blessed his community in many ways with this wealth. His company has given millions to a local private Christian university, thousands to a Christian youth center, supported a pro-life pregnancy center and donated to Christian films.

The going wasn't always easy for Jim. It took time to build the prototype of his compressor; conflicts among partners had to be solved; there were government regulations that had to be followed that would delay progress and many other things that were obstacles to overcome to make the company successful. Jim even tells of the difficult challenge he personally faced learning to be a businessman when all of his training was in engineering. The important thing is that he was persistent. He never gave up. He and his family have been rewarded for it and the community blessed because of it.

Vince and Jim are two examples of how persistence works in the secular world, but there is a roll call of believers in the Bible and in history that provides evidence that persistence is essential for success in the calling that God gives each individual. The shining example from the Old Testament is Joseph, Jacob's favorite son.

The Faith of a Dreamer

I once wrote a small book on Joseph entitled, *Club Joe*. The phrase means that you can join Club Joe if you have adverse experiences in life like Joseph, but find that these experiences are used by God to put you in a place where he can richly bless you so you in turn can bless others.

The fact that Joseph was Jacob's favorite son did not go unnoticed by his ten older brothers. Jacob sent Joseph to check on his brothers who plotted to kill him when they saw him coming. Reuben prevailed on the others not to kill him so they threw him in a pit then sold him off to some Ishmaelites on their way to Egypt. This was a horrendous injustice Joseph experienced, but it would not be his last. He was sold in Egypt to one of Pharaoh's officials and in this man's service, Joseph proved himself to be a valuable asset. He became the chief-operating officer of the Egyptian noble's household. Joseph lived up to the meaning of his name, "Increase."

Joseph stayed true to his faith in God. The Scriptures say: "[3] When his master saw that the Lord was with him and that the Lord gave him success in everything he did,[4] Joseph found favor in his eyes and became his attendant. Potiphar put him in charge of his household and he entrusted to his care everything he owned." (Genesis 39: 3 and 4)

Joseph must have voiced his faith in God because the Egyptian took note how skillfully Joseph worked and how trustworthy he was. Joseph was making wealth for his master and giving a witness for his God at the same time. No doubt Joseph held on to the hope that his master would be so grateful that he might be released one day to return home.

The handsome Joseph caught the eye of his master's wife who tried to seduce him. Joseph stayed true to his God and rejected her sexual advances. However, he became the victim of this desperate housewife as she falsely accused Joseph of forcing himself on her. Joseph once again endured injustice as he was wrongly placed in prison.

Incarceration did not weaken Joseph's faith. He was persistent in serving his God. His character trait of trustworthiness was seen by the warden who then trusted Joseph with the care of the prisoners. He went from number two in Potiphar's household to number two in the prison. While in captivity Joseph had interaction with two other prisoners who had been engaged in royal employment. The Pharaoh's cupbearer and baker were fellow inmates. Each of these men had dreams that Joseph was able to interpret. Joseph had favorable news for the cupbearer but the opposite for the baker. The former would be restored to his position, but the latter would meet an unpleasant execution.

Joseph asked the cupbearer to remember him to Pharaoh so he could be released since he was unjustly placed in the dungeon. The scriptures say that the cupbearer forgot about Joseph but God did not. There is also no evidence that Joseph forgot about God or turned from him in disappointment. God had his perfect timing in place. When Pharaoh had a troubling dream, it jogged the cupbearer's memory. Joseph was quickly collected and brought before Pharaoh to explain the dream.

Joseph understood that there would be seven years of prosperity followed by seven years of famine. You are likely familiar with the story and know that Joseph became number two in command of Egypt under Pharaoh. I wonder how Potiphar's wife felt about all these happenings. Two years Joseph waited for that cupbearer to help spring him from prison. This had to be a real test of faith during this time. Joseph held true and his faith was persistent, and now he was where God wanted him.

Joseph as number two in Egypt did not have an easy time of it. He was in charge of putting grain in storehouses for the coming years of famine. There had to be those who opposed this policy and wanted to benefit from their seven bumper crops. No doubt there were Egyptian nobles whose agricultural wealth was hurt by this young Hebrew, ex-slave, and ex-con who was now giving them commands.

Joseph's position was instrumental in saving his family. The famine also hit hard in Canaan causing his brothers to come to Egypt to buy food. After various encounters, Joseph revealed himself to his brothers and in Genesis 50:19-21 we read some of the most beautiful words in the Bible:

> [19] But Joseph said to them, "Don't be afraid. Am I in the place of God? [20] You intended to harm me, but

God intended it for good to accomplish what is now being done, the saving of many lives. ²¹ So then, don't be afraid. I will provide for you and your children." And he reassured them and spoke kindly to them.

The beauty of these words is that Joseph shows that he is the fusion of faith and forgiveness. He was persistent in his faith and hoped that he would see his family again. He never gave up and an amazing result took place. We must believe that God is in control. Even when injustice scores a hit on us, if we are persistent in our faith and keep working at the task God has given us, he will make us overcomers.

Seeking a Man in Macedonia

The hero of persistence in the New Testament is the Apostle Paul. He is the twelfth apostle, but his only time with Jesus was a brief miraculous encounter on the road to Damascus. It is astonishing that the one apostle who did not travel with Jesus during his earthly ministry has written more of the New Testament than any other of the eleven apostles. The book of Acts, which is the early history of the church, devotes more time to Paul's ministry than all of the other eleven disciples combined.

When Saul met Jesus Christ on the Damascus Road, he was given an assignment at the time of his conversion. He was to proclaim "Christ to the Gentiles and their kings." He went from persecutor Saul to missionary Paul.

One incident in Paul's ministry that gives insight into his tremendous spiritual character happened on his second missionary journey. He and his traveling companions had been kept by the Holy Spirit from preaching in the province of Asia. They then sought to enter Bithynia which is the northern part of today's Turkey but the scriptures say, "… the Spirit of Jesus would not allow them to." (Acts 16:7) Paul ended up in Troas where he had a vision of a man in Macedonia who was begging him to come to his area. Paul and his group quickly made their way to the town of Philippi in Macedonia.

This is all very significant. Paul had personal plans for ministering, but he believed they were not endorsed by the Holy Spirit. He waited until God gave direction to Macedonia. Paul was persistent to seek God's will, and once sure of it, immediately complied. Paul's travel to Macedonia was the first time the message of Christianity was taken to the continent of Europe. This very historic moment was the result of Paul's obedience to the leadership of the Holy Spirit.

Paul came to the city of Philippi where he shared the message of Christ with a business woman named Lydia who traded in purple cloth. She and her whole household were converted and baptized.

Paul then encountered a slave girl who was possessed by a spirit that gave her the ability to tell the future. Paul commanded the evil spirit to come out of her and she was free. Those who profited by the girl's actions moved against Paul and his companions. They were attacked, beaten and thrown in prison.

You would think that Paul might have second guessed himself. Maybe he had misread God's will. Maybe he shouldn't have come to Macedonia because it did not turn out well. Maybe the vision was just a bad dream. Paul and Silas did not opt for a pity party, but instead spent the time praying and singing hymns. An earthquake loosened their chains and opened the doors. The jailer arrived and in despair prepared to take his own life. Paul restrained him saying that all the prisoners were still present.

The jailer must have known about Paul's activity in town and his message. He said to Paul and Silas, "Sirs, what must I do to be saved?" (Acts 16:30) The jailer and his household became Christians. Paul had found the man in the vision to be the jailer. The first church in Europe was born. Paul did not lose faith when it appeared his ministry was stopped by incarceration. He stayed persistent in his faith. God came through, making his position in a prison the ideal place for him to fulfill God's will.

Paul and Silas were released and asked to leave peacefully but Paul refused because they were Roman citizens and had been jailed without a trial. This news frightened the authorities and they came to appease Paul. He and Silas went to Lydia's house and had a church service before they left town.

Paul encountered many adverse circumstances in his ministry that would make men of lesser character throw in the towel. Paul persevered in God's will. He knew what his mission was; and he believed God would provide what he needed to fulfill it. Paul shared with the Corinthians some of the difficulties he had endured in his ministry:

> [24] Five times I received from the Jews the forty lashes minus one.[25] Three times I was beaten with rods, once I was pelted with stones, three times I was shipwrecked, I spent a night and a day in the open sea, [26] I have been constantly on the move. I have been in danger from rivers, in danger from bandits, in danger from my fellow Jews, in danger from Gentiles; in danger in the city,

in danger in the country, in danger at sea; and in danger from false believers. [27] I have labored and toiled and have often gone without sleep; I have known hunger and thirst and have often gone without food; I have been cold and naked. [28] Besides everything else, I face daily the pressure of my concern for all the churches. (2 Corinthians 11:24-28)

Paul counted the suffering for sharing the gospel all worthwhile in order to see people come to Christ. He was not going to let anything stop him from doing the task God put before him. He clearly expresses this in 2 Corinthians 4:7-12:

[7] But we have this treasure in jars of clay to show that this all-surpassing power is from God and not from us. [8] We are hard pressed on every side, but not crushed; perplexed, but not in despair; [9] persecuted, but not abandoned; struck down, but not destroyed. [10] We always carry around in our body the death of Jesus, so that the life of Jesus may also be revealed in our body. [11] For we who are alive are always being given over to death for Jesus' sake, so that his life may also be revealed in our mortal body. [12] So then, death is at work in us, but life is at work in you.

The Apostle Paul knew very well the value of persistence. He gave illustrations from athletics and the military where persistence is essential to victory. Paul wrote, "Everyone who competes in the games goes into strict training. They do it to get a crown that will not last, but we do it to get a crown that will last forever." (1 Corinthians 9:25) He encourages his protégé, Timothy, to endure suffering like a soldier, "Join with me in suffering, like a good soldier of Christ Jesus." (2 Timothy 2:3)

Paul's testimony of faith reveals his consistency and persistence to his Lord, "For to me, to live is Christ and to die is gain" (Philippians 1:21).

A Force against Slavery

One of the darkest times in the history of western civilization was during the African slave trade. It was not only an issue that scarred America, but also was a serious problem for Great Britain and was out of harmony with Christian values. While America was emerging as a new independent nation on the world stage, a young man in England was emerging as a force for freedom for those who were victims of the atrocity of slavery.

William Wilberforce became the embodiment of persistence for the task God laid on his heart. He was an MP, a Member of Parliament. Early in his political career, he believed that slavery was a practice unsuited for civilized people, and he dedicated himself to make it illegal in the British Empire.

In 1784 he became an evangelical Christian and thought he might best serve as minister. He was influenced by his minister friend, John Newton, to stay the course as an MP and fight to end slavery. This issue was dear to the heart of Newton, who before his conversion and call to the ministry, served as a captain of a slave ship. This abhorrent iniquity burdened Newton so adamantly that the forgiveness he found in Christ inspired him to write what could arguably be called the most famous hymn of the Christian faith, *Amazing Grace*.

God confirmed Newton's guidance. Wilberforce immersed himself in the fight to end the slave trade. Political struggles are prone to be long, especially when powerful people have financial interests at stake. Wilberforce found this out to his own personal disappointment but still he persisted because he believed it was God's will. Year after year he would bring his bill forward and debate its merits and see it voted down.

Finally, enough change in attitude and circumstances favored the bill. In February 1807 the bill passed ending the slave trade, a victory that opened the possibility for total abolition in the future. Three days before his death, Wilberforce learned that concessions were made that guaranteed passage of the Bill for the Abolition of Slavery.³ He died on July 29, 1833 and was honored with an interment in Westminster Abby.

Wilberforce was persistent in the mission God gave him. He never quit even when the political tide and personal health issues worked against him. The battle was long but the victory saved countless lives, the number known only to God.

The Father of Modern Missions

You most likely have heard a missionary to some foreign land speak in your church or you may have attended a missionary conference where a number of missionaries were present. Hopefully, you have made a monetary contribution to mission work. In all of this you are participating in the movement started by a man who lived at the same time as Wilberforce.

William Carey was also a subject of the British crown but ventured far from his English homeland to be a missionary to India. For his vision, initiative, faith and relentless persistence he has been given the title of the "Father of Modern Missions." Carey believed that God's mission for his life was to take the gospel to India. Doing mission work in India today is no easy task given the culture, the number of religions practiced and the many languages. Imagine what it must have been like for Carey and his family in the 19th century.

The culture was totally different from England's. A caste system determined economic status and many other aspects of life. Such a system was totally adverse to Christian standards. If a Hindu became a convert, the new Christian had to consider how it would affect his or her caste position.

Since he was doing a relatively new thing in the Christian faith by going out as a missionary, financial support was lacking from home. To solve this problem, he became manager of an indigo factory. While serving in this position, he completed the revision of the Bengali New Testament during his free time.

His early days in India were not happy ones from a personal standpoint. One son died of dysentery and his wife suffered a nervous breakdown from which she never fully recovered. The work was hard and progress was slow. It took Carey working persistently for seven years before he had his first convert. How many of us would have surmised that this lack of success was a sign to apply our talents elsewhere?

Carey had a gift for learning languages. For thirty years he was a professor of Indian languages at Serampore College. Besides being faithful to his teaching duties, he translated the Bible into Bengali, Oriya, Marathi, Hindi, Assamese, Sanskrit and parts of it into other dialects and languages spoken by the people of India. One cannot overestimate the value of a person reading the Bible in their own language.

Many feel that the greatest legacy Carey gave the people of India was these many translations of the Bible into the vernacular.[5] His work in this area was very beneficial to future missionaries who would later serve in India. Sitting at a desk translating scripture can a lonesome and tedious job that does not generate the public adoration common for a visible evangelist, but Carey was persistent to the work and India is the richer for it. His famous quote is "Expect great things from God and attempt great things for God."[4]

Carey died in 1834 at the age of seventy-two. He served in India for forty-one years without a furlough. He only had 700 coverts but many thousands would later accept Christ because of his translations.[5] This prime example of persistence served his Lord well in a hard place with many obstacles. Every successful missionary from his time until now has gone forth with the heritage of vision and steadfastness displayed in William Carey's life.

A Champion for Children

If I were asked the question, "How do you know that God is real?" I would answer, "Because of the life of George Muller." His name is synonymous with Christian orphanage ministry, in which he excelled in Bristol, England in the 1800s. He was originally from Germany, born Johann Georg Ferdinand Muller in 1805. His biography by Roger Steer had a far- reaching spiritual impact on my life.

His father hoped George would become a clergyman and thereby gain a comfortable life. Muller's youthful days saw him engaged in a lifestyle that gave no indication that Christian ministry was in his future. Gambling and drinking were common ways for him to spend his time. One evening, he happened to attend a prayer meeting that became the turning point of his life. Soon after this meeting he knelt by his bed and became a believer in Christ.

In 1829 he found work in London with The London Society for the Promotion of Christianity Amongst the Jews. He later felt called to Bristol to partner with his friend Henry Craik at Bethesda Chapel. Muller was a gifted preacher and large numbers attended his services. It is amazing how God will sometimes lead someone into a work that they never aspired to do, but circumstances clearly revealed God's will making that work their special calling. This is how it was with Muller and his orphanage work.

When he first arrived in Bristol, he was deeply touched by the plight of children begging in the streets. He could see that the need was great and that something needed to be done. Much praying and planning took place before the first children's home run by Muller opened in Bristol on April 11, 1836.

He persistently followed God's leading in this ministry down through the years dealing with the problems of relocation, increase of children, building of new facilities and all the problems associated with the expenses of running such an operation. None of these problems derailed him from the mission. He was faithful to the task and persistent in his passion and work for the physical welfare and spiritual life of the children in his care.

The needs of the children were great and always present. George Muller had a very unique means of acquiring the financial resources for the orphanages, prayer. It sounds so simple and a bit unreasonable, but it is completely true. When it came to spiritual persistency, George Muller was consistent and persistent in prayer. All financial income was a result of prayer, persistent prayer.

Sometimes meeting the daily need for the orphanage was in doubt, but prayers were answered and funds would come in the mail. Someone would stop by and reveal how God told them during their morning devotions to bring a donation of money.

Muller has stated that there were times when the needs were very dire and funds very low, but the children in the orphanage never knew of the seriousness of the situation. They never felt in want. Muller's pray-it-in policy resulted in many camouflage miracles that benefited them.

Muller's success gained him much attention and the usual critics that come with this territory of notoriety. There were those who said that his funding came in because he was a foreigner or that his work was an attractive novelty or the result of his annual reports being published. Muller responded to his critics:

> My being a foreigner, looked at naturally, would be more likely to hinder my being entrusted with such large sums than to induce donors to give. As to novelty procuring the money, the time is long gone by for novelty, for this is June 1856 and the work commenced in March 1834. As to the secret treasure to which I have access, there is more in this supposition than the objectors are aware of;

> for surely God's treasury is inexhaustible, and I have drawn that (though that alone) to go to, and have indeed drawn out of it, simply by prayer and faith, more than £113,000 since the beginning of the work.[6]

As to his published reports on the work, Muller attributed any donations that might have come in as the work of the Lord moving on the donor who read the report. In his own words, Muller gives his reason for his funding procedure, "My chief object was the glory of God, by giving a practical demonstration as to what could be accomplished simply through the instrumentality of prayer and faith …"[7]

Muller did not need the professional fundraiser, the slick marketing direct mailer, or the skillful development director. He just needed persistent prayer and a belief that God would come through to meet the needs. I have the feeling that if I were to visit George Muller in heaven, I would find his mansion in a gated community.

Real prayer that touches the heart of God is the hardest spiritual discipline to master. George Muller made his whole ministry and life dependent on it. Later in life, he preached around the world with a visit to the United States that included an invitation to the White House. He even traveled as far away as Australia which was no small feat for an aging man in the days before auto and jet travel. Muller lived to be ninety-three years old and worked in ministry until his last day. He is truly one of the remarkable men in the history of Evangelical Christianity.

His astounding legacy includes the care of 10,024 orphans, establishing 117 schools and educating more than 120,000 children. Thousands around the world were also converted under his preaching.

I could add to these all-stars of faith from history some contemporary figures. Mother Teresa's work in India among the poor was extraordinary. Franklin Graham has given a new dimension to his father's organization of ministry outreach through the benevolent work of Samaritan's Purse. Dr. James Dodson, a psychologist with a Ph. D. in Child Development, who founded and led Focus on the Family has had a positive impact on many families providing them hope and ways to establish a spiritual foundation in their homes. All of these are examples of the quality of persistence for successful ministry.

When we compare ourselves with these heralded Christian servants, we are inclined to regard ourselves as totally inadequate or extremely inferior. You can rest assured that each of these heroes of the faith had their times of spiritual struggle and times when they needed God to renew their fervor for their mission.

Learning from a Fearful Prophet

If you feel that you have some short comings in spiritual persistence, do not despair. Reconnect with God in prayer and renew your commitment and faith to be steadfast to the task to which he has called you. Recall the story of the prophet Elijah, which is recorded in 1 Kings Chapter 19. Elijah had just experienced a fantastic victory over the prophets of Baal at Mount Carmel where God blessed his sacrifice with fire, after which he put Baal's prophets to the sword.

The Queen Jezebel put a death decree on Elijah so he turned tail and ran. He was holed up in a cave on Mount Horeb having a self-pity party. Instead of his faith being strengthened by the hand of God giving him a great victory, he was afraid for his life because of the word of an evil queen. God decided to have a session with the prophet:

> [11] The Lord said, "Go out and stand on the mountain in the presence of the Lord, for the Lord is about to pass by."
>
> Then a great and powerful wind tore the mountains apart and shattered the rocks before the Lord, but the Lord was not in the wind. After the wind there was an earthquake, but the Lord was not in the earthquake.[12] After the earthquake

came a fire, but the Lord was not in the fire. And after the fire came a gentle whisper. ¹³ When Elijah heard it, he pulled his cloak over his face and went out and stood at the mouth of the cave.

Then a voice said to him, "What are you doing here, Elijah?" (1 Kings 19:11-13)

Sometimes we become discouraged as we seek to fulfill the work God gives us. As we sit in the cave of discouragement, we need to hear the Lord say to us, "What are you doing here?" Oswald Chambers said, "Discouragement always comes when we insist on having our own way."[8]

Elijah was told to get back at it. He obeyed and followed the Lord's direction. We need to do the same. We need to stop sulking in the locker room and get back on the field knowing we have a God that comes through when we persevere for him. We have to remember that when God is on our side, we are not at a disadvantage.

The Christian walk does not go down Easy Street. If you are involved in serving God in a ministry or special task you will encounter adversity at some point in time, especially if your work is getting the gospel message to unbelievers.

No Promotion from God's Will

When I was a young pastor back in the 1970s, my wife and I went to a district event to hear an invited speaker preach what has been termed the "Health and Wealth" gospel. We both left feeling there was a crack in the bell. What was conveyed is not something that our denomination ever had emphasized. The speaker claimed that it was God's will for us to live in health and wealth.

He went on to say that we should have faith for this and take bold steps. We should tithe on what we would like to make instead of what we actually made so God would be obligated to give us more money and our tithe would still equal ten percent. I have known people who have been healed of sickness but I have also preached the funerals of those who were not. In the suffering of their last days, they still praised God and were a witness for him.

I have known people whom God has blessed with wealth and they have been generous with it. I have also known medical doctors who could have remained in America and gained wealth, but instead they followed God's will to the mission field making less than many high school grads in America.

In James' epistle we see there is value in the trials we encounter in our Christian walk and ministry. James 1:2 and 3 reads, "² Consider it pure joy, my brothers and sisters, whenever you face trials of many kinds, ³ because you know that the testing of your faith produces perseverance." Our trials help us to be persistent.

When I was in seminary, I had a Church History professor named Mendell Taylor. I learned much about church history from him, but the most fascinating thing I learned in the class came from one of his opening class prayers which I still remember some fifty years later. In his prayer he said, "Lord, we know there is no promotion from the will of God." Think about that, "No promotion from the will of God." That means the bishop and the church janitor stand on equal ground if both are in God's will.

We are to press on persistently in the face of trials because if we are in God's will, there is no better place where we can be. Sometimes God may release you from one assignment to another. As long as you are sure in agreement with the Holy Spirit that the new task is God's will, then you are not only free to accept it, you must accept it to stay in his will.

Another "p" word you need to be acquainted with is "patience." Patience is not something many of us do well.

We live in the age of microwaves, fast food restaurants, automatic teller machines, jet travel and an email that takes seconds instead of days to reach its receiver. When we are faced with a problem and are wondering what to do, sometimes the answer is "do nothing except wait." "Wait" is a four letter word that most of us don't like, but often that is how God works in our best interest. The Psalmist writes, "Wait for the Lord; be strong and take heart and wait for the Lord" (Psalm 27:14). Following God's will is tough at times, but we should always be encouraged, because we have read the end of the book and we win! The words in 1 John 4:4 should encourage us, "…the one who is in you is greater than the one who is in the world."

James also provides words that can help us stay the course: "Blessed is the one who perseveres under trial because, having stood the test, that person will receive the crown of life that the Lord has promised to those who love him" (James 1:12).

Discussion Questions: Chapter 2 Persistent

1. Has God made clear to you what his will is in service or ministry to him? How are you dealing with it?

2. Share an incident when you encountered a problem or difficulty as you sought to do God's will in serving him. How did you cope with it and how did it affect you.

3. In the story of Joseph of the Old Testament, what stands out to you as the most remarkable thing about his life?

4. Paul's plans were interrupted by the leading of the Holy Spirit. Have you ever had God interrupt your plans? If he has, describe the situation and tell what you learned from it.

5. Three heroes of the faith are introduced in the chapter, Wilberforce, Carry and Muller. Which of these three impressed you the most with their perseverance doing God's will? Share the reason for your choice.

6. What lesson is to be learned from Elijah as he went from great victory to fear and

discouragement? What is to be learned from how God spoke to him? What modern day parallels are there to this story?

7. James tells us that we should expect trials to come our way as we serve the Lord. What does this say about the reality of living obedient to Christ? How should we prepare for these trials?

8. What did you discover in this chapter about your walk with Christ that you would like to improve? What actions would be helpful for you to take?

3

Resistant

Standing Strong against Temptation

The "R" in *CPR for Believers* stands for "Resistant." In sports there is a saying, "Defense wins championships." In the area of persistence, we looked at executing the mission God gives us to do. That is us on offense, trying to advance God's kingdom. We must realize that as we seek to take the message of Christ forward, there is an enemy who is pushing back. Satan is this enemy. He relishes the possibility of us falling away and leaving the mission of Christ as we yield to his temptations.

Trouble for the First Couple

When you become a Christian and start on your journey of discipleship, the devil will do his best to get you back. Whether you were conscious of it or not, he had you before you chose Christ. Satan successfully targeted

Adam and Eve, the crowning work of God's creation. The first couple was created in a sinless state but with a free will. Satan tempted them to use that free will to disobey God. Adam and Eve were free to eat from any tree in the garden except the one in the middle of the garden.

When Satan came to Eve, she told him that this tree was off limits. Touching or eating from it would result in death. Satan's means of temptation is worth examining. We read in Genesis 3:4 and 5, [4]"You will not surely die," the serpent said to the woman. [5]For God knows that when you eat of it your eyes will be open, and you will be like God, knowing good and evil."

What the devil puts before Adam and Eve is not rebellion against God, but the opportunity to be like God. This does not seem undesirable. In fact, it appears to be a step up. The lie in all of this was that they were already like God having been created in his image and living free from sin.

The temptation that Satan brought was not to rebel against God, but to be selfish and move to the same level as God. Most of the temptations that come our way are the same. Satan does not want us to rebel against God or hate him; just do something that pleases the self.

Mark this, Satan wants you. If Satan thought he had a chance of getting to a sinless Adam and Eve, do you think he is going leave you alone just because you have accepted Christ as your Savior? You still have a life tainted by the fallen nature, passed down from Adam and Eve. You are a weaker target than the first man and woman were. As you live the Christian life, Satan will target you. 1 Peter 5:8 sounds a clear warning, "Be alert and of sober mind. Your enemy the devil prowls around like a roaring lion looking for someone to devour."

Satan prowls like a lion to seek our spiritual destruction, but we have the "Lion of Judah" on our side who is the real Lion of strength. If we submit ourselves to this Lion who is Jesus Christ, we have the resource to withstand the evil attacks that come our way. James 4:7 says, "Submit yourselves, then, to God. Resist the devil, and he will flee from you."

Notice that it first says, "Submit yourselves to God." If we do this, we have the means to resist the devil. Our success in resistance is tied to our connection with Christ. If we have been consistent in our relationship with Jesus and persistent in following him, then he will provide us with the power to resist the temptation that Satan brings our way. This verse of Scripture has a positive ending, because the devil is said to flee from us when we resist.

Old Testament Failures

The Bible contains stories of people who succumbed to temptation. In Joshua Chapter 7, we learn of the sin of Achan, a solder in Joshua's army. Joshua was greatly distressed because Israel lost a battle that they should have easily won. God guided him in how to discover the one who had disobeyed and whose sin brought this defeat. Tribes, clans and families were ordered to pass by in front of Joshua while God indicated the link to the guilty one. Joshua confronted a man named Achan who confessed:

> [19] Then Joshua said to Achan, "My son, give glory to the Lord, the God of Israel, and honor him. Tell me what you have done; do not hide it from me."
>
> [20] Achan replied, "It is true! I have sinned against the Lord, the God of Israel. This is what I have done: [21] When I saw in the plunder a beautiful robe from Babylonia, two hundred shekels of silver and a bar of gold weighing fifty shekels, I coveted them and took them. They are hidden in the ground inside my tent, with the silver underneath." (Joshua 7:19-21)

The soldiers had specific instructions not to take any of the plunder in the previous battle. Achan could not resist the temptation to do so with horrible consequence for the army and his own family as the biblical account attests in later verses.

Another more familiar Old Testament character also failed to resist temptation was King David whose wandering eyes led him to be snared by temptation of the evil one. The account is given to us in 2 Samuel 11:1-3:

> In the spring, at the time when kings go off to war, David sent Joab out with the king's men and the whole Israelite army. They destroyed the Ammonites and besieged Rabbah. But David remained in Jerusalem.[2] One evening David got up from his bed and walked around on the roof of the palace. From the roof he saw a woman bathing. The woman was very beautiful, [3] and David sent someone to find out about her. The man said, "She is Bathsheba, the daughter of Eliam and the wife of Uriah the Hittite."

David was not where he belonged. Kings went off to war with their armies in the spring. This time David stayed behind. He was not following the mission God gave him as king and leader of the army. He was showing signs of not being consistent and not being persistent. If you fail at maintaining consistent fellowship with the Lord and fail to be persistent at your God given task, then you are in no position to successfully resist when temptation comes.

David succumbed to the lust of his eyes and acted out on it as only a king could do. It was a national scandal and a deep personal sin that caused David much personal regret. He was made painfully aware of his sin and the damaging extent of it by the prophet Nathan. His journey back to God was a hard road to walk that included the death of two sons.

New Testament Failures

The New Testament provides examples of those who failed when faced with temptation. Acts Chapter 5 gives the story of Ananias and Sapphira, a husband and wife who sold a piece of land and brought the money from the sale to the church to put in the donation box. They sought credit for making a 100% donation of the money gained from the sale. God revealed to Peter that this was not true. Peter called Ananias out on it. This deception cost Ananias his life. His wife met the same fate some three hours later after repeating the same lie.

One of the saddest stories in the New Testament is that of a young man named Demas. He was a young protégé of Paul much like Timothy. He and Timothy were most likely acquainted and friends. They may have even shared conversations of how exciting it was being prepared for ministry by the wonderfully gifted and insightful Paul. The apostle signs off his letter to Philemon declaring Demas as a fellow worker.

However, there is another verse that mentions Demas in 2 Timothy 4:10, "for Demas, because he loved this world, has deserted me and has gone to Thessalonica." Demas had left Paul for the pleasures of this world. Demas willfully deserted Paul and the mission. He could not maintain persistence and was therefore too weak to resist the temptations that the world had to offer a young man. I have always thought if Demas had stayed true to the work and God's will for his life, there would have been another New Testament epistle to Demas to impart more enriching insight of the Christian faith.

Sin in the Christian Community

The two sins, stealing and wrongful sex, were tragic for Achan and David. I have known of Christians removed from their position at a church or Christian organization because they were guilty of misusing funds or outright embezzlement. The sin was painful for them and embarrassing for their families. I have known pastors who have lost their credentials because of sexual immorality. There have even been Christian leaders with national celebrity status that have failed in this area. It is not only the leaders of the faith that encounter this enticement, but many in the ranks of the laity face it as well.

A number of years ago I produced a documentary video entitled, *Every Young Man's Battle*. It was based on the bestselling book by the same name and featured the authors of the book. The video and the book focus on the topic of pornography which has seeped its way into the Christian community more deeply than we care to admit.

The film reveals that the average age a boy sees his first porn film is eleven. I have more recent statistics now that puts the age at nine. David's path to sexual sin was a view from his palace balcony. Today it only takes a few clicks on a computer mouse.

These kinds of sins do happen in the Christian community, but they are not as prevalent as the secret sins that trip up so many Christians today. The fact that the sins can be kept secret make them all the more difficult to deal with since they are hidden from a caring friend who might be of help. These are more dispositional sins than outright acts of sin. If the Ten Commandments form our categories of sin, these sins would fit under "Thou shall not covet."

One can covet and no one else can know. Coveting does not give off a sound nor is it visible to the eyes of others, because it is a sin held under guard in the heart. It is a sin so subtle that sometimes it takes a good bit of time to recognize it is there. There is the old saying, "The grass is greener on the other side of the fence." For many Christians the thought is, "Life is better in someone else's skin." Satan likes to come around and drop his little whisper bombs in our brains so they will explode in our hearts. You may have encountered some of these bombs:

- He is so lucky to have that good job, how did he ever get it? I'm way more talented.
- Her husband sure treats her better than mine.
- I wish my kids were turning out as good as theirs.
- How come I wasn't chosen for the *O Holy Night* solo?
- Why can't we afford a vacation trip like they took?

I could go on and on. Items like this can infiltrate your life and fester for months, maybe even years, and no one will know but three persons – You, God and Satan. The latter will be absolutely thrilled with the situation.

These sins in attitude are like a cancer to the soul that slowly eats away at one's spiritual fiber until there might be an outward appearance of Christian faith while none really exists. You will recall in the chapter on consistency that daily consistent connection with Christ is foundational. Every Christian becomes more vulnerable to temptation when a daily connection to Jesus is ignored or neglected.

I know this to be true from personal experience and likely you could affirm the same. When I have gone astray from the faith, it has been during times when I have not kept the connection with Christ consistent. When not consistent, I am not persistent and then I am vulnerable to the temptations that can walk into my life wearing sneakers.

I was involved in a project of which I was the writer and main financier. I partnered up with an organization that had the technical equipment and expertise to make this video a great success. The premiere was held at a church and was wonderfully received. Later, before the project was released to the public on a major scale, I discovered that the organization had reedited the film and took full credit for the copyright and even changed some of the scenes without my approval.

I was deeply hurt that an organization using the word "Christian" in their name could do such a thing. We were on the verge of legal proceedings when a settlement was reached where my name was returned to the copyright and the original editing restored.

The issue might have been regarded as solved, but it continued to gnaw at my inward spiritual life. I was wronged and did not like it. I was not able to muster the "locked in faith" that Joseph of the Old Testament demonstrated as described earlier. It was a sin easily hidden in public, but it did not make my home life a pleasant everyday experience as my wife could attest. Those silent secret sins that eat away at our souls, which we give sanctuary in our hearts, do as much damage to our relationship with Jesus as any acted out sin.

If hatred is harbored in the heart, it does more damage to you than to the one to whom your displeasure is directed. The one you despise may not even know you still hold a grudge and have moved on with their life, but you are still in a spiritual spiral downward. I was able to gain victory over this sin of wrong attitude when I surrendered it to Christ and asked for and received his forgiveness. I am glad that I learned this lesson, because similar challenges would confront me in the future.

We must remember that Christians are human and humans will disappoint. Disagreements will emerge, but they need not destroy your relationship with Christ. Some Christians will never have peaceful, joyous and victorious lives until they bring their sins of attitude to the Master and ask for his forgiveness.

These sins are dangerous because they can be accommodated while you still play the role of the believer. You can still perform your church responsibilities whether it is serving on the board, teaching Sunday school or singing in the choir, but God's anointing and blessing will be absent. You will be performing duties but not serving the Savior. The outward acts of sin might be easy to resist but the sins that would claim us as a host that can be effectively covered are more difficult to repel, and Satan knows this.

The Bible lets us know what Christians are up against in Ephesians 6:12: "For our struggle is not against flesh and blood, but against the rulers, against the authorities, against the powers of this dark world and against the spiritual forces of evil in the heavenly realms."

In Christ, we stand opposed to the "powers of this dark world" and against the "forces of evil in the heavenly realms." We are involved in spiritual warfare. Satan is on the attack. He seeks your weakness then designs a temptation to cause your fall. Jesus told Peter that Satan wanted to sift him and the other disciples like wheat (Luke 22:31). In Jesus' day wheat was shaken in a fan or sieve and the chaff thrown off. Satan would love to so shake the life of any Christian to have them be separated from Christ and their faith thrown off.

In chapter ten of 1 Corinthians, Paul gives his readers a history lesson of when the children of Israel were on their Exodus from Egypt and broke with God, falling into sexual immorality and pagan revelry. As a result, God sent venomous snakes and many were bitten and died. Moses crafted a bronze serpent for the people to look upon if they were truly sorry for their sin and wanted to repent. Those who looked upon it were saved. This is why the emblem of medicine today has a snake spiraling around a pole (Numbers 21).How could they have fallen into sin? They had experienced the miracle of the Passover in Egypt and the miraculous deliverance through the Red Sea, yet still they failed to resist temptation from the evil one.

It was in this context that Paul said to the Corinthians in 1 Corinthians 10:12, "So, if you think you are standing firm, be careful that you don't fall!" He was warning them that if those who followed Moses, saw all the wonders God did to get them out of Egypt, and still were overcome by temptation, then they also should be on guard even if they think they are standing firm. Paul wanted them to know that they could be vulnerable if they became slack in their consistent fellowship with Christ. Satan would still have a go at them if he thought there was a possibility of them yielding.

The apostle Peter endorses Paul's warning. 2 Peter 3:17 states, "Therefore, dear friends, since you have been forewarned, be on your guard so that you may not be carried away by the error of the lawless and fall from your secure position." To be on your guard is a military reference, which conveys this concept of resistance. A palace guard was expected to put up a resistance to any unwelcomed intruder. We are to be prepared to resist Satan's advances.

The Need for a Shield

In Ephesians 6:13-17, Paul presents his analogy of the armor of God in our spiritual war. He mentions the "breastplate of righteousness," the "shield of faith," and the "helmet of salvation." All three of these items are for defense. Our spiritual warfare encounters requires preparation with strong defense with which we can resist our enemy. A warrior with a sword and no shield is at a disadvantage. You may have good skills and great talent to use in serving the Lord, but if you have not prepared a spiritual character to withstand the attacks of Satan you are in danger of falling in the battle.

Danger in the Culture

Cultural trends are another cunning method Satan uses to trip up Christians. We have a natural tendency to want to fit in and not be the odd ball. God wants us in the world but not of the world. Some believers find this hard to discern. When the entertainment industry and a news media promote favoritism for something that is clearly denounced in Scripture, it can lead to confusion and vulnerability for Christians who are not well versed in the Bible.

The "same sex marriage" issue is one such item. Linked to it is the homosexual lifestyle that is considered an abomination in the Old Testament and also condemned in the New Testament. In Leviticus 20:13 same gender sex is called detestable and was for the Hebrews a capital offense. Paul shares God's displeasure of the homosexual lifestyle in Romans 1:26-28, "and that they were given over to a depraved mind."

He later states to the Corinthians that those practicing homosexual acts will not inherit the kingdom of God (1 Corinthians 6:9-11). According to the Pew

Research Center, 36 percent of evangelical Christians say homosexuality relationships should be accepted.[1]

This means they do not regard it as a sin. In no way should any Christian harbor malice to any homosexual. The saying, "Hate the sin, love the sinner," is suitable. I have interacted with homosexuals in some of my secular work positions and they have always treated me with respect and I have done the same to them.

They knew that as a Christian I could not condone their lifestyle, but neither could I condone the lifestyle of the people who worked with me that were cohabitating or engaging in adultery. God's standard is "no sexual immorality" which means sex is only to take place between a man and a woman who are married to each other.

This is not my made-up rule. It is what the Bible proclaims. A Christian who wishes to be consistent in a relationship with Christ, persistent in service to him and resistant to temptation will obey this absolute. Paul says in Ephesians 5:3, "But among you there must not be even the hint of sexual immorality, or any kind of impurity, …" The words are plain and the standard is high. It is set by God. The temptation to go along with the popular trend in culture is strong, but it must be resisted. If we doubt or distrust the Word of God, then our faith is in serious jeopardy.

The Galatians were being led astray on doctrinal issues. Paul had difficulties with people who undermined his ministry to the gentiles. They would preach that to be a true Christian you still had to follow all the Jewish laws. This infuriated Paul who wrote in Galatians 3:1 "You foolish Galatians! Who has bewitched you? Before your very eyes Jesus Christ was clearly portrayed as crucified." Paul wanted the Galatians to trust in the atonement of the crucified Christ for their redemption and not feel they needed to add a burden of laws to make their salvation complete.

There are two colleges in the rural Ohio county where I live. One is an evangelical church supported university where my wife and I worked. The other is a liberal arts college that can even boast of a U. S. president (Hayes) as one of their alums. My wife came out of retirement and worked at this college as a part time librarian while they sought to hire a permanent one. It is a prestigious private college that attracts students from all over the country. We have friends who work there.

This college has extended us a fantastic benefit since we live in the village of its location. We have a membership to their state-of-the art athletic facility that has basketball courts, tennis courts, an indoor track, competitive swimming pool and a weight room. We paid less for a lifetime membership than what most people pay for a monthly fee at their exercise gym. I am so grateful for this opportunity that I donate facial tissues in the winter time and the students readily use them.

One day I was walking in for my workout and saw a bumper sticker on a car in the parking lot. It had the words, "Prayerfully Pro-Choice," and the logo of a church denomination was beside them. Psalm 139:13 says, "For you created my inmost being; you knit me together in my mother's womb." This verse of the Bible reveals that God is involved in the development of an unborn child. Anyone who engages in performing an abortion is directly doing battle with the Creator of Life. God seeks to form a child in partnership with the mother and an outside force dares to come in and stop the work of these divine hands.

The Bible also shows that the prophets Jerimiah and Isaiah were called to their missions when in the womb. The biblical evidence is that God sees the unborn as a person. One Christian denomination believes it is acceptable to take a position more aligned with pop culture or more suitable to their political leanings than what evidence is provided by Scripture. To be sure, this denomination would not be listed under the evangelical category, but still it claims a position in Christianity.

If Paul were alive today, I think he would have one of his assistants fire off an email to this denomination and say, "Who has bewitched you?" Any church or Christian that does not base their beliefs on the Word of God is like a ship without an anchor that slowly drifts in despair on the sea destruction.

We have to resist being pulled to false doctrines that are unsupported in the Bible even if they appear to fit more comfortably in the culture in which we live. There are no shortages of false doctrines to sway Christians today. We need to stand firm and resist the temptation to depart from God's Word.

Staying True to God's Will

Polycarp was a second century bishop of Smyrna. He may have been the disciple of John the Apostle who ordained him to this position. The emperor of Rome decided to crack down on Christians because they refused to worship the Roman gods and the emperor's image.

Polycarp was taken prisoner and given a chance to recant his faith for his life. The elderly Polycarp made the following response, "Eighty-six years have I served him, and he never did me any wrong. How can I blaspheme my king who has saved me?" He was then burned to death.[2] Polycarp resisted the pressure to deny his faith in Christ even though it meant his death.

We should not be surprised that temptation comes our way because even our Lord had to face it. In Matthew Chapter 4, the account of Jesus being tempted by Satan is provided. The laughable temptation was when Satan showed Jesus all the kingdoms in their splendor and said, "All this I will give you if you bow down and worship me."

Some 30 years earlier Jesus had left the glories of heaven to be born in a stable. He knew he would return back to heaven someday. Satan was showing him a world that Jesus created. Satan's appeal to self-glory fell flat because Jesus was all about doing the will of his Father in heaven.

The true temptation of Jesus was not with the devil in the desert. It was alone in a garden called Gethsemane. Jesus prayed, "My Father, if it is possible, may this cup be taken from me. Yet not as I will, but as you will" (Matthew 26:39).

According to many Bible scholars, what Jesus wanted to avoid was not the suffering or the crucifixion, but instead that moment when he became the sin of the world on the cross and his Father had to turn his holy eyes from his Son who was now the sin offering. This is why on the cross Jesus said, "My God, my God, why have you forsaken me?"(Matthew 27:49) This was the only time in eternity that God the Son and God the Father were ever separated. It was our sin that separated them. Jesus loved us so much that he was willing to be our sin so when God had to turn his eyes off his Son, it made it possible for God to turn them back on us if we accept Christ's atonement for our sins.

The door of salvation is open to us because Jesus Christ resisted the temptation to avoid the separation from his Father so he could be our sin offering. This should inspire our desire to resist temptation. We have no excuse for yielding to temptation because we have the resource to win over it. Paul told the Corinthians (1 Corinthians 10:13):

> No temptation has overtaken you except what is common to mankind. And God is faithful; he will not let you be tempted beyond what you can bear. But when you are tempted, he will also provide a way out so that you can endure it.

We have the promise from God in his Word that he will provide a way out of temptation. If we fail to resist what Satan brings our way it is totally on us, not on God. In the next chapter, we will learn how we can effectively execute life changing CPR for Christian living. God has richly provided all we need for us to be consistent in connecting with Jesus, persistent in following his will and resistant to Satan's temptations.

Discussion Questions: Chapter 3 Resistant

1. James 4:7 says, "Submit yourselves, then, to God. Resist the devil, and he will flee from you." What do you believe is involved in this action of submission?

2. Describe the steps that led to King David's failure and what were the tragic results? What could parallel this in our times and culture?

3. Demas deserted Paul and left the Christian faith. Many young people are doing this today. What are some of the reasons why this is happening? How can the trend be reversed?

4. The chapter talks about the sins of attitude. Have you ever had a problem with them and how did you deal with them? How can the church address secret sins?

5. We live in a permissive society with a culture that does not embrace Christian values. How shall Christians live in this situation and develop defenses to keep it from pulling them down while executing positive actions to present the life changing message of Christ?

6. Staying true to Christ in the face of persecution can be a daunting task, especially if your life is on the line. What would a Christian need to have in order to cope with such a situation?

7. How can a Christian best defend against temptation?

8. What did you discover in this chapter about your walk with Christ that you would like to improve? What actions would be helpful for you to take?

Application

Utilizing the Divine Guidance System

I entitled this last chapter "Application" instead of "Conclusion" because my hope is that you will apply the content to your life according to your need. A conclusion where you simply come to the end of another book and toss it aside would miss the purpose of these pages. All of us need to improve in the Christian life. Focusing on the areas of consistency, persistence and resistance are three good places to examine as we take self-spiritual inventory.

I chose "Application" because "Apps" are so the thing now days. We have our smart phones and our favorite apps on them. Hit an app and find the weather. Hit an app and see how your sport team is doing. Check on your Facebook app and see what your friends are up to, or post something yourself so the world can know what you are experiencing. You can even hit an app and have a Bible verse come into view and expand to more verses. I like this one myself. There are all kinds of apps for the phone and the computer. The word "app" is short for "application." The makers of the app hope we will apply the app to our lives and believe that such an application is beneficial.

Our Own Personal Guide

Success in being consistent, persistent and resistant as described in the previous three chapters is a daunting task for us to take on individually. We need the help of the Holy Spirit. Jesus tried his best to explain it all to his disciples before his crucifixion, but their minds were not in a place to fully comprehend it. Later, it would all make perfect sense when they had their unique experience at Pentecost. He said:

> [5] but now I am going to him who sent me. None of you asks me, 'Where are you going?' [6] Rather, you are filled with grief because I have said these things. [7] But very truly I tell you, it is for your good that I am going away. Unless I go away, the Counselor will not come to you; but if I go, I will send him to you. [8] When he comes, he will prove the world to be in the wrong about sin and righteousness and judgment: [9] about sin, because people do not believe

in me; ¹⁰about righteousness, because I am going to the Father, where you can see me no longer; ¹¹and about judgment, because the prince of this world now stands condemned. (John 16:5-11)

The word "Counselor" is translated "Advocate" in other editions of the New International Bible. The King James Version uses the word "Comforter" and the New American Standard Bible uses the word "Helper" as does the Phillips New testament. What term is used is not important. What is important to know is that Jesus promises not to leave us alone as we navigate the sea of life as his followers.

A spiritual miracle takes place whereby Christ puts his divine nature inside of us through the Holy Spirit. Remember the verse 2 Peter 1:4, "Through these he has given us his very great and precious promises, so that through them you may participate in the divine nature, having escaped the corruption in the world caused by evil desires." The way we participate in the divine nature is by having the Holy Spirit in our lives.

If you were to go on safari in Africa or climb a challenging mountain like Everest, you would be offered a guide and be wise to accept. This is what Jesus does with the Holy Spirit. He gives us our personal guide for our spiritual trek in life. In John 16:13, Jesus says, "But when he, the Spirit of truth, comes, he will guide you into all truth."

Paul fully understood what Jesus said about the Holy Spirit living in us and guiding us. He states, "⁵Those who live according to the sinful nature have their minds set on what that nature desires; but those who live in accordance with the Spirit have their minds set on what the Spirit desires. ⁶The mind of sinful man is death, but the mind controlled by the Spirit is life and peace" (Romans 8:5 and 6).

The Holy Spirit resides in our hearts but he works through our minds as we live out the Christian life. This makes sense because the actions we make first go through our minds. If you commit a willful act of sin, your mind first had to approve it. If you let your mind be controlled by the sinful nature, then your mind will support and lead you into sin. If your mind is controlled by the Spirit, then you will seek to be Christlike in your actions.

In Romans 12:2, we read, "Do not conform to the pattern of this world, but be transformed by the renewing of your mind. Then you will be able to test and approve what God's will is—his good, pleasing and perfect will." Paul is telling us that we need to have a mind overhaul so that we can discern the perfect will of God. The way we have our minds renewed is to have them controlled by the Holy Spirit.

Living Two Days at a Time

It is unproductive and frustrating to God if we live our lives in inconsistency. One day we are controlled by the Spirit then we hit a spiritual snag and go back to being controlled by the sinful nature. It is that elevator experience where we move up and down in a close relationship with our Lord. This does not help the kingdom of God and it does not help us if we live this way. In Fact, it is downright dangerous with eternal consequences.

Joshua said, "…choose for yourselves this day whom you will serve … But as for me and my household, we will serve the Lord" (Joshua 24:15). Notice that he says "this day." In reality that's the way it is; we make a choice every day who we will serve. Satan is ever hopeful that he can put something desirable in front of you to get you to choose him for a day. If your mind is controlled by the Spirit, the choice is joyfully made for Jesus Christ.

Sometimes when you ask someone how they are getting along they may answer that they are just living one day at a time. It is a logical answer since we only get one day at a time to live. My concept of this was changed by a German monk named Martin Luther who rocked the world some 500 years ago when he nailed ninety-five theses on the Wittenberg church door.

Luther's philosophy was that you lived only for two days. He said, "There are two days in my calendar: This day and that Day."[1] "This day" was the actual date of the day being experienced and "that day" was the day he would have to face God or Judgement Day. There is an old hymn I remember singing in church. It was entitled, *I Know Whom I Have Believed.* Here is the refrain in the song:

> But "I know Whom I have believed,
> And am persuaded that He is able
> To keep that which I've committed
> Unto Him against that day."[2]

It is a song of faith which believers sing as a testimony that their faith is in Christ and that they are confident of their salvation in him because they have given their lives over to him and are "all in". Many of the old hymns have sound theology which we would be well served to revisit from time to time.

The Strange Fisherman

The late Dr. Robert Schuler during his successful days as the pastor of the Crystal Cathedral in Garden Grove, California would host pastor conferences. As a young pastor in the 1970s I attended one. During one of the lunches my table was right behind the table where

Dr. Schuler was sitting so that there was a small space between our backs. I boldly slid my chair back and got the famed minister's attention. I said, "Dr. Schuler, have you heard about the man who had a photographic mind but only turned out negatives?" This guru of possibility thinking formed a wide smile and replied, "Oh, that is so good. May I use it?" It was my honor to grant his request.

I tell this story because I am going to use one of his. I heard him speak once about an odd fisherman. The angler was strange because he immediately measured every fish he caught. He pulled in his first catch and measured it. It was 12 inches long and he threw it back in the water. Second fish measured nine inches and he kept it. Another fish was 14 inches long so back in the water it went. An eight incher was reeled in and kept. A tourist was watching and he finally asked the fisherman why he threw the big fish back in the lake and kept the smaller ones. The fisherman relied, "You see it's very easy to explain. My frying pan is only ten inches wide."

A chuckle filled the room. Then Dr. Schuler said, "Do you know who that fisherman is? It is likely someone in this room." The chuckles went silent. He went on to say that many people have thrown away the great opportunities God has put before them because they did not think they had the talent, resources or whatever to successfully complete them.

If God calls you to do something and you know it is definitely from God, then to refuse is to walk away from the will of God, which is always a danger for a Christian. God is more concerned about our availability than our ability. He will always provide what we are lacking. Our responsibility is to be faithful.

Jor-El Godsey is the President of Heartbeat International, one of the leading pro-life organizations in the world. I have become acquainted with him through my work in the pro-life movement. One time our paths crossed at a conference in Michigan where he was the featured speaker. He said one line that made the conference all worthwhile. His words were, "Everything you want in life is on the other side of ..." I was sure he would say 'the fence. " he did not. Instead the full statement was "Everything you want in life is on the other side of fear." Fear is the invisible wall that Satan uses to keep us captive in self-pity, self-centered focus, a false sense of inadequacy and a host of other destructive items which prevent us from successfully executing CPR for a victorious Christian life.

Fear is a Liar

My wife had surgery for diverticulitis. She was very concerned because she does not do well in surgery recovery. The anesthetic and medications reap their havoc. She prepared herself mentally and spiritually by listening to a song on her smart phone entitled, *Fear is a Liar* by Zach Williams. Jesus said in John 14:1 and 2, [1] "Do not let your hearts be troubled. You believe in God; believe also in me. [2] My Father's house has many rooms; if that were not so, would I have told you that I am going there to prepare a place for you?" The King James Version translates rooms as mansions. This formed the basis for another song by the 2nd Chapter of Acts entitled, *Mansion Builder*. Annie Herrings lyrics are both inspiring and comforting:

> So why should I worry
> Why should I fret?
> 'Cause I've got a Mansion Builder
> Who ain't through with me yet[3]

I heard a preacher once define worry as "putting the car in neutral and stepping on the gas." It makes a lot of noise and gets things on the inside moving, but it doesn't get you anywhere. Paul writes some of the most powerful inspiring words of the Bible in Romans 8:15-17:

> [15] The Spirit you received does not make you slaves, so that you live in fear again; rather, the Spirit you received brought about your adoption to sonship. And by him we cry, *"Abba,* Father." [16] The Spirit

himself testifies with our spirit that we are God's children. [17] Now if we are children, then we are heirs—heirs of God and co-heirs with Christ, if indeed we share in his sufferings in order that we may also share in his glory.

God's Best Offer

The late Creath Davis was a Christian author and speaker who wrote a phenomenal book entitled, *Beyond This God Cannot Go*. This scripture reveals the best offer we have in life; God cannot make a better one. We are taken into his family as his sons and daughters whereby we become co-heirs with Christ. Jesus suffered and died on the cross so we could share the glory of heaven for all eternity as his co-heirs.

This is full complete redemption. We have the Holy Spirit so we do not have to live in fear. If we are bound by fear, then we'll not have a consistent relationship with Christ. We'll be too scared to be persistent in our service for him. We'll have already established that we are not able to resist a favorite ploy of Satan which he loves to use to trip Christians.

The disciples knew that Jesus was resurrected. They had met with him and fellowshipped with him, but they were no force to be reckoned with after their Lord returned to the Father until Pentecost. They were told by Jesus to wait for this time when they would receive the Holy Spirit. The Spirit totally transformed them from fear to power. They boldly took the redemptive message of Jesus Christ to the people who just weeks before called for the crucifixion of their Master. Many people that day put their faith in Jesus as the Messiah.

Martin Luther, John Wesley, George Whitfield, Charles Finney, George Muller and other all-stars of the faith have had that special experience beyond their initial encounter with Jesus when they were forgiven of their sin. They had that" A-ha" moment when they became all-in for Jesus through the Holy Spirit. Some call it sanctification; others refer to it as the deeper life experience. I don't want to split theological hairs but to make the point that this experience equips us with the power to live our lives in a spirit of Christlikeness where we can be consistent, persistent and resistant. We then serve unselfishly the Son of God who desires to share his inheritance with us. As we serve, his kingdom advances, and as we remain in him, we bear much fruit.

Victory through Surrender

How one obtains this experience is described by the author, missionary and evangelist E. Stanley Jones. This

Methodist minister spent time as a missionary to India. He has provided some of the best spiritual insight that a Christian could ever receive to foster Christian maturity. He wrote a very provocative book entitled, *Victory Through Surrender*. This title at first glance seems illogical, but in a closer look it makes all the sense in the world. He reveals the heart of his book in these words:

> The difference between the emphasis on self-realization or on self-surrender seems to be this: in self-realization you try to realize yourself, for all the answers are in you. In self-surrender you surrender your self to Jesus Christ, for all the answers are in Him. One leaves you centered on you – a self-centered and self-preoccupied person, albeit a religious person. The other loses his self and finds it. For self-realization only comes through self-surrender. You realize your self when you surrender to Him.[4]

When you make your surrender in a similar way you find your forgiveness from sin. You pray in believing faith that if you surrender to him all that you are, he will give to you all that he has promised. You willingly become all-in so he can be, through the Holy Spirit, all in you. Jones later in his book wrote, "Christianity is not a philosophy or a moralism to be learned. It is a Lord to be surrendered to and to be obeyed."[5]

Don't let a misstep or failure cause you to give up. David, after his sinful scandal, came back to where God referred to him as a man after his own heart. I have known ministers who have fallen in disgrace who have come back to once again lead ministries blessed by God. CPR for the Christian life as a believer can remind you of your need to be steadfast and faithful. It will be helpful for you to do a spiritual check up with the Lord in your personal worship time where you check on how you are being Consistent, Persistent and Resistant as you walk with him.

All my years as a minister I have heard preachers call for revival to the extent that it would be a Third Awakening in America. I would love to see it happen and feel our nation is overdue for such a movement of the Spirit of God. I do not think it will happen until Christians in our churches confess and seek forgiveness for the secret soul eaters, those sins of attitude that are easily cloaked in our hearts.

As I look at these three words of consistent, persistent and resistant I believe they are the foundation stones for success in all areas of life, be it sports, business, family life and other areas. There is no better place to utilize them than in the Christian Life. If you would like to make that surrender to Christ today, simply pray the prayer below in faith that God will meet your need and fulfill his promise.

Dear Lord, I totally surrender my complete life to you. Take control of every aspect of my life. Guide me by your spirit so I may always stay in the center of your will. Guide my steps in your way and if I dare to stray, have your Spirit check me and keep me on the path of righteousness. Teach me to love you with all my soul, heart, mind and strength. Give me the desire in my heart to be your true disciple. Give me the desire to develop a consistent relationship with you. Help me be determined to persistently serve you. Form within me the character to resist the temptation to move from you. I ask this believing that you want to give me your Spirit and your brotherhood. Amen.

If you prayed this prayer or in some way have been helped by this book, please visit our website at **www.lifechangingcpr.com** and share your story.

Discussion Questions: Chapter 4 Application

1. The Holy Spirit is described as Counselor, Comforter and Helper. Which of these three is most meaningful to you and why?

2. Paul speaks of the "renewing of your mind." Why is this important for a Christian and how does it take place?

3. The Holy Spirit is the spiritual guidance system given to us by Jesus. How has the Holy Spirit guided you in your Christian walk?

4. Share a time when you were faced with a task that took you out of your comfort zone and even made you fearful when dealing with it. How did you face it and what helped you through it?

5. Many great Christians throughout history have had that special experience beyond their initial encounter with Jesus. Has this happened to you? If it has, please describe it.

6. E. Stanley Jones' book, *Victory Through Surrender*, at first glance seems to convey an illogical thought. Why is this so and why

should it be instead considered basic to the Christian faith?

7. As you self-examine your life, which of the three, Consistent, Persistent or Resistant, is the area to which you need to give the most attention to maintain a victorious Christian life?

8. What did you discover in this chapter about your walk with Christ that you would like to improve? What actions would be helpful for you to take?

Notes

Chapter 1 - Consistent

1. Kyle Idleman, *Not a Fan*, Zondervan, Grand Rapids, Michigan, p. 32.

2. Francis Chan, *Crazy Love*, David C Cook, Colorado Springs, CO, p.69.

3. Chan, p.72.

4. Chan, p. 75.

5. Chan, p.77.

6. Chan, pp. 90-98.

7. Richard A, Swenson, MD, *Margin*, NavPress, Colorado Springs, CO, p. 121.

Chapter 2 – Persistent

1. Annie Herring, *Takin' the Easy Way*, song is by 2nd Chapter of Acts and appears on the album *Singer Sower (1983)*. © Sparrow Records.

2. https://www.vinceflynn.com/about-vince

3. Hague, William (2007), *William Wilberforce: The Life of the Great Anti-Slave Trade Campaigner*, London: Harper Press, p. 502.

4. Yeh, Allan; Chun, Chris (2013). *Expect Great Things, Attempt Great Things: William Carey and Adoniram Judson, Missionary Pioneers*. Wipf and Stock. p. 117.

5. https://www.christianitytoday.com/history/people/missionaries/william-carey.html

6. Roger Steer, *George Müller: Delighted in God*, Christian Focus Publications, Great Britain, 1997, p. 123.

7. Steer, p. 131.

8. Oswald Chambers, So *Send I You*, Discovery House, 1930, p. 170.

Chapter 3 - Resistant

1. Caryle Murphy, "Most U. S. Christian Groups Grow More Accepting of Homosexuality," December 18, 2015, *Pew Research Center, Fact Tank*, http://www.pewresearch.org/fact-tank/2015/12/18/most-u-s-christian-groups-grow-more-accepting-of-homosexuality/

2. William J. Petersen and Randy Petersen, *The One Year Book of Psalms*, 1999, Tyndale House Publications, Wheaton, IL, Entry for June 1.

Chapter 4 - Application

1. Martin Luther, *The Bondage of the Will*, 1525.
2. Daniel Whittle, *I Know Whom I Have Believed*, pub. 1883, public domain.
3. Anne Herring, *Mansion Builder*, Latter Reign Music, 1978.
4. E. Stanley Jones, *Victory Through Surrender*, Abington Press, Nashville, Tennessee, 1966, p. 8.
5. Jones, p. 64.

Acknowledgements

I am grateful to my friend, Dr. Bruce Petersen, who reviewed the manuscript and made such wonderful comments that they became the Foreword of the book. His wife, Jackie, read it by her own choice and made very encouraging comments for which I thank her. I appreciate all those who wrote endorsements. They all live very busy lives and it is indeed a labor of love for them to take time to review the pages and write supportive comments. I owe much gratitude to my wife, Edythe, who was my number one supportive fan on this project and my editor-in-chief.

www.ingramcontent.com/pod-product-compliance
Lightning Source LLC
Chambersburg PA
CBHW052059070526
44584CB00017B/2253